COLORS

a

poetry

anthology

by Kira Winter

Printed in the USA by IngramSpark.

For information about stockist orders,
fulfillment, special discounts, bulk
purchases, or author events, please contact
Kira Winter at kira.c.winter@gmail.com.

Artwork, illustration, and book design
by Lucia Gaia. www.luciagaia.com.

The typefaces used in this book are
KG HAPPY and Gooper Text.

The illustrations for this book were
rendered using Adobe Fresco.

First edition.

ISBN: 9780578337548

to my butterfly

may
your wings
span eternity

COLORS

KIRA WINTER

contents

LOVE

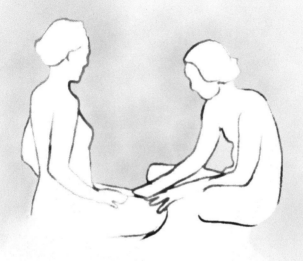

give me
a million versions
of reality
and i'd find you
in every
one.

– fate

i was a traveler.
a wanderer.
a nomad.

always searching –
forever unsettled.

then i met you

and
nothing
feels aimless,
as it did before.

– *home*

the
weight
of the world
has felt light

ever since
i held
your heart.

– *light*

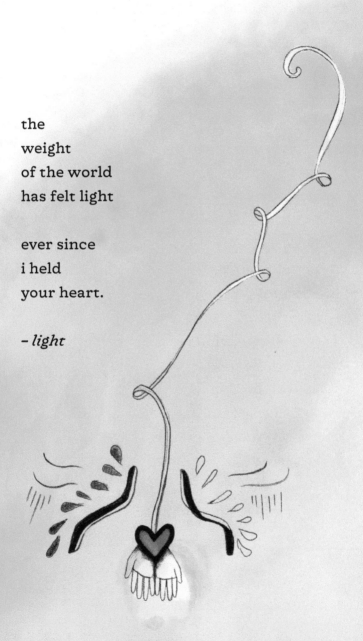

i'll take my love
reckless,
with a touch of insanity.

reckless –
like we're standing
on the edge
of the golden gate.
hands clasped,
swaying
with the winds
and the swells
and the birds.
hearts pounding
each time one of us
gets too close
and forgets
just how high we are.

insane –
as in, i lose
myself to you.
awaking every morning
unsure of who i am
because you've
molded me
into something greater
than i ever could have been
alone.

i'll take my love
reckless,
with a touch of insanity,
because anything less
is an injustice
to us.

– *reckless love*

the
shine
of her smile.

the
warmth
of her eyes.

i
am
the seedling,
experiencing spring,
for the very first time.

– *seedling*

you light me up

like
the ocean
lights the sky.

move me

like
the moon
moves the tide.

– *light me up*

let's love
like the stars

shine
through the ages

radiate
with such brilliance,
even time doesn't dare
change us.

let's dance
with the tides

sing
with the sea

stare
wide-eyed to the sky,
til we drift
off to sleep.

let's shout
to the gods,
so they look
down
and smile.
envious
of our innocence,
if only
for a while.

– *whimsy*

my
firefly
in the day

just
waiting
til the night

so,
the
world

can see you —

as i do.

– *my firefly*

a
rose,
by any
other name,
would be
yours.

– *shakespeare's flora*

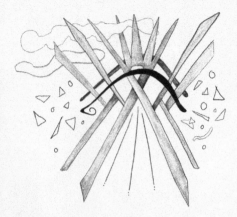

she has
kaleidoscope
eyes.

illuminating
pink
to fire
to orange

every sunrise.

– *kaleidoscope eyes*

come as you are

my sun
moon
or
star.

your shine

will
always
be welcome.

– come as you are

she whispers –
my mellifluous.

he doesn't
know
what it means.
but the way
she says it,
sounds
so
sweet
and light
and smooth,
he never
had to
ask.

– *mellifluous*

what if
heaven and hell
is here?
the subtle distinction,
whether you're near.

what if
darkness,
isn't dark at all?
just light, patiently,
awaiting your call.

what if
i,
had never found you?
would love be a lie,
and truth be untrue?

– *paradise personified*

i'd call you
my love

but that feels
too short,
too tired,
too inadequate
a description
of what you mean
to me.

could i then
hold you
as an idea?

this too –
feels stunted.

for an idea
can exist
in the abstract,
and i've encountered
nothing in life
more real than you.

no.

you
are just,
you.

indescribable.
undeniable.
true,
as true.

– *inarticulable*

LOSS

if
love
is a travesty,
i want
to be
devastated.

– *travesty*

i won't
call myself a saint,
or paint the past
anything
less
than black.

but i gave
you
a piece of me.

and even though
i searched,
and searched,
i could never seem
to find it
again.

i'm not asking
for it back.

just
wondering,
whether you kept it.

– piece of me

she felt splintered.

torn
between
the growth
she could
see

and the growth
she could
be.

– *splintered*

i
feel
numb today.

like
all life's colors
just slipped away.

leaving
roses and skies
and ocean blue eyes,
shallow, hollow, and gray.

– colorless

i'd tell you
what a beautiful day it is.
i'd tell you how
the white snow clouds
against the blue lit sky
revitalizes this belief
that humanity
is somehow distinct.
then again, most days are beautiful,
so you probably already know this.

i'd tell you
how gorgeous you are.
i'd tell you that if
i hadn't woven my fingers
through your cinnamon warm hair
i could have never
fully appreciated desire.
then again, you're always gorgeous,
so that seems counterproductive.

i'd tell you
how you mean more to me
than anyone else could.
i'd tell you how
heaven is simply a place
where i'm given the opportunity
to make you happy.
then again, you're happy now,
and i'm alone.

so, i sit in silence.

reminiscing
over unspoken words,
and left with only
the belief
that nothing positive,
is ever counterproductive.

– *silent renaissance*

like a
helium balloon
she lifts and floats and soars.
until one day,
she doesn't
anymore.

– *helium*

as
the sun
fades from grace
and night takes
its place

i can't help but wonder —

why
are the
darkest times,
always alone,
in my own mind?

– *nightfall*

what can i say?

i'm
damaged.
i was born damaged.
and loving me,
there will be consequences.

of course: we will love.

the type of love
that ignites
a civilization,
burning it to rubble
so it can be built anew.
the sort of love
that strikes
like lightening,
causing your heart
to never beat the same.

but know this: you will hope.

the same hope
god feels
for her fallen angels.
aware how it ends,
even god, still prays for change.

but why?
why.

i'm damaged.
let it go.
let me destroy
someone else.
i just don't want it
to be you.

– *damaged*

the roses aren't
red,
they're black
and they've died.

the violets, never
blue,
more clear
have they cried.

the love
that we had,
never true—
only lies.
built
to wilt,
like hope
in the night.

– *a flower's death*

there are times
when people are in love,
and there are times
when people are not.

but what happened to us?

how did we become
stuck in the middle,
somehow doing
both,
and neither,
all at once.

– *purgatory*

he was like an ocean.

and i,
so very thirsty,
drank and drank and drank.
never understanding
why my desires
felt unquenchable.

– *salt*

i know
some things
are better left
unsaid.

i just wish
these weren't
the same things,
that needed
to be.

– unsaid

his tears
became memories,
and his memories
became dry,
fractured.

he looked at her
one last time
mustering
a final, broken question:

"when will i heal?"

she didn't
have the heart
to tell him,
sometimes you don't.

– *scars*

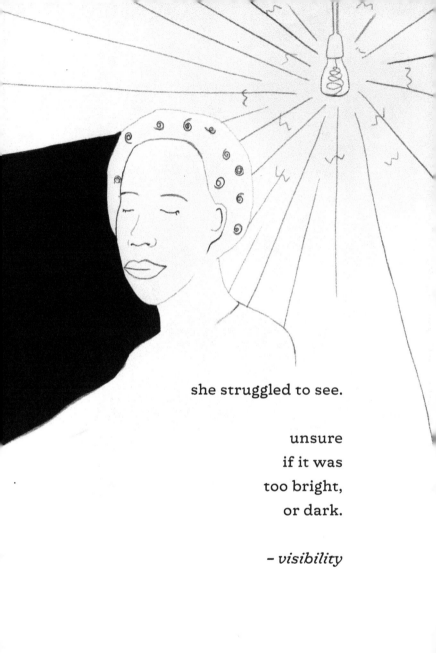

she struggled to see.

unsure
if it was
too bright,
or dark.

– *visibility*

we train
all our lives
to prepare
for the noise.

but are left,
utterly unequipped,
when confronted
with silence.

– *restless*

HOPE

focus on love.

all
else
flows
naturally.

– love's trajectory

she stares at the stars,
imagining each fiery, little pearl
is an unseen dream
she cannot wait
to one day
meet.

what she does not know
is the stars themselves
stare back down
at her.
mesmerized
by her radiance,
and each pleading
to become the dream
she one day follows.

– *starlight sonata*

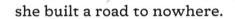

she built a road to nowhere.

knowing
even the most
deserted and desolate
of places

held
their own
hidden oasis.

– sanctuary

as
the
flower

tilts
to
the sky,

so do i.

– love's lean

how many nights
have i opened the sky
and dreamt
of what i would do?

how many days
have i risen from dreams
but felt
they'd never come true?

now, in peace,
i rise
and sleep
for fate
has given me
you.

– *risen in peace*

with enough time,

all
things
may grow.

but with enough love,

this
same
growth,
becomes limitless.

– limitless

she stood like a statue
as life
battered
and berated
and whittled her away.

but little did life know,

years
of anguish
only managed
to produce a masterpiece,
that all the worlds would marvel at,
forever and ever and ever.

– masterpiece

be
the flower
that blooms
where
none other could.

– eureka dunes evening primrose

you show me
color
without light.

give me
poetry
without words.

grant me
vision
without sight.

teach me
love,
can be deserved.

– *affirmation*

the sun
and her eyes
spoke sunrise
to mine.

the moon
and her smile
moved mountains
not tides.

and i, just a traveler,
with a few words
and rhymes.
spent eternity
in this moment,
even heaven
couldn't design.

– the sun and her eyes

she
held
that same
shock and awe
of thunder and lightning.

– electrifying

love will grow.

sometimes
it ignites
as a scorching inferno
where heat and passion and fervor
fuse in elation.
other times
it flickers
from timber to timber
lighting ablaze
an uncontrollable kindle.

however,
never compare
the ignition to the inferno.
just trust in chemistry –
and love will grow.

– *chemistry*

how
do you
take
my breath
away,
and yet,
still
help me breathe.

– oxygen

and in that moment

where
the voices wilted
and the choices bloomed

she realized
hope,
had never
abandoned her,
after all.

– renewal

the romantic, she never dies.

with grim
in her eyes,
and recklessness
as her nature,

she confronts –

shoot coward,
you'll only
make
me,
a legend.

– *immortal*

EARTH

our
roses
rust to gold,

our
corals
bleach to bone...

when
will we see
how we've
tainted
our native jewelry?

– *bleached*

i glanced at the sun
but did not go blind.

i walked through the flame
but suffered no burn.

i stretched for the tree
but she shied away.

i grabbed at the earth
but she was cold
and damp.

against the stillness,
she had left.

i was alone.

– *alone*

i wonder -

when the last oyster shell dissolves

will
the rich
now starve
with the rest of us
all?

– *dissolution*

the mountain, she groans,
as rich soil
critters and oil,
are stripped away,
are mined for pay.
seam by seam,
ton by
ton.

the tree, she weeps,
as lush leaves
forest and seeds,
are cleared round,
are cut down.
root by root,
acre by
acre.

the ocean, she shrieks,
as vibrant coral
creatures and floral,
are bleached to death,
are put to rest.
reef by reef,
sea by
sea.

the sun, she says nothing.
simply stares
down in sadness.
knowing
she once gave life
to all creation,
and now counts celsius,
to extinction.

– if the silent could speak

she awakens to the sounds of
silence.

where
the birds
are all voiceless,
and the ocean
lies still.

she wonders –

when we will see
we are the meteor
hurling to earth.

– *meteor*

be as three;
the soil, grass and sun.

and, as one;
this harmony,
of give and take,
that weaves us as none.

– equilibrium

her knuckles
ripped and tore
as she pulled out
the last withered crop.
she looked over
her dry, deserted farm,
and sighed.
the last of its kind.

his lips
cracked and split
under the sun.
he dipped his pole
into the rusting
ocean depths below.
unsure why.
he hadn't seen life
in several days,
and the fish just seemed
to make him sicker, anyway.

her body
cramped and chilled
as she lay in bed
trying to be still.
it was too hot to move.
too hot inside.
too hot outside.
these days
even the shade,
it sweltered.
she tried to cry
but there was
no water left
for tears.

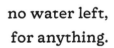

no water left,
for anything.

the man,
he just sulked.
god had promised him
a glorious end,
an apocalypse.
but it seems
god had decided
to take everyone,
but him.

what he misunderstood,
was god played no role
in man's extermination.
to the contrary,
man was perfectly competent
to achieve that goal,
on its very own.

– *the last of us*

hope is not lost

but it is
becoming
harder
and harder
to believe.

– *fade*

i'm sick and i'm tired of <u>resiliency</u>.

they say our earth will persevere, for she is
<u>resilient.</u>

they say humans will endure, for we are
<u>resilient</u>.

they say animals will adjust, for they are
<u>resilient</u>.

while i appreciate the beauty of
adaptability, will there ever be a time again
for progress? or are we fated to forever
remain on the brink of annihilation, where
saving the status quo - <u>remaining resilient</u>
- is our only attainable achievement?

– *brink*

listen –
hear her roar.
as she orchestrates
from the heavens
down, to the ocean floor.

listen –
hear her plea.
as she holds
on to hope
doing anything, to be seen.

listen –
hear her sigh.
as she fades
like cooling embers
waiting, to die.

listen -
hear anything,
anymore?

– *listen*

she begged –
can you see
how i'm stripped,
whipped and scarred?

but he
shut his eyes
let the world
turn to dark.

she pleaded –
can you hear
as i weep
of eternal loss?

but he
filled his mind
with such racket,
all was lost.

she cried –
you must feel
how i boil
and yet, freeze.

but he
felt nothing
unless pure
ecstasy.

now
here he sits –
blind, deaf and numb.
appreciating
warmer weather,
unconcerned
of all to come.

– blind, deaf and numb

even if climate change is wrong,
it doesn't make the maltreatment
of our earth
right.
it doesn't make it just.

as humans,
we tend to think
things are only good
when they are good, for us.
when they can be used, by us.
as the self-proclaimed
creators of value
without us,
everything must be,
valueless.

but if we created value
then we created
other concepts as well:

<u>the precautionary principle</u> –
because we cannot know
the full effect of our actions.

<u>unnecessary waste</u> –
because using something
for no reason, feels wrong.

<u>eudaimonia</u> –
because a life well lived
is a life lived with balance.

<u>altruism</u> –
because our greatest acts
are the selfless ones.

even if climate change is wrong.
even if we aren't in the 7th great
extinction.
even if none of this matters.
because nothing has value
unless we give it –
our actions are still unjust.

we simply violate
too many other
abstract,
human created
principles.

– *stewards*

she waits –
quietly; maimed.

wondering
whether
to ever create
again.

- *mother earth*

WONDER

to write
is to set forth
something
out into the world
that never could have
existed,
if not for
you.

that,
by itself,
is extraordinary.

– *the beauty of you*

breathe in this moment

it
has
to last
a lifetime.

– exhale

are we
so different
from sunflowers?

chasing warmth
and rays.

trying to grow
more than we wilt
day
after day.

- *my sunflower*

she sits
at her desk
scribbling of
hope and love
justice and nature.

people misunderstand her.
say she's bi-polar
and about as consistent as
dr. jekyll.

for on one day,
she writes as if angels
descend on snow white clouds.
and on others,
like she's describing
different shades of darkness,
but focused on one,
darker than all the rest.

but what they fail to see,
or perhaps, can't.
is she writes not of herself.
but of you.
and of me.

when women are trafficked;
she is violated.
when refugees lose hope;
she is hopeless.
when animals go extinct;
a piece of her, is lost forever.

so, you see, she is no jekyll.
to the contrary,
she appears to be
the sanest,
of us all.

– jekyll's angel

the poem began as the poet

without
rhyme
or
reason
and just a splash
of anarchy.

– *poet's piece*

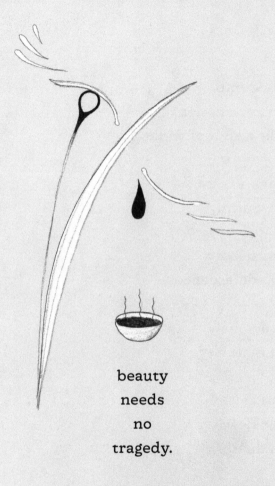

beauty
needs
no
tragedy.

– light can shine without darkness

we
succumb
to our opinions,
like a shot of vodka.

recklessly
in youth.

cautiously
in adolescence.

graciously
in maturity.

and
recklessly
in death.

– *succumb*

i've heard that time
heals all wounds.

but i wonder –

if wounds
are continually
self-inflicted

isn't time
just another
predicate,

for pain?

– *volition*

you
don't
have to have
problems,

to know sadness.

– you know you

there are
wolves.

and there are
sheep.

but i am neither,

who am i?

– *i am me*

we don't love
mandela
for eradicating racism.

nor kant
for resolving ethics.

we love them,
for attempting
to do so.

when an act
presents itself
as impossible.
always remember
the attempt
is wholly in your power.

– no road is linear

was
he
scared

or
scarred

did it matter?

– *forward*

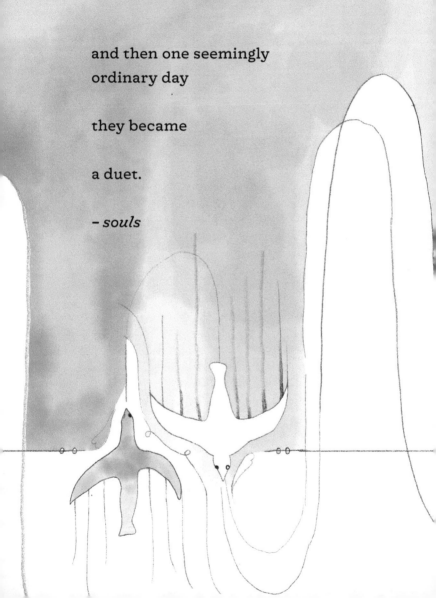

and then one seemingly
ordinary day

they became

a duet.

– *souls*

must
all love

shatter

before
it ever feels
whole.

- pieces

meeting you
was like meeting
oblivion.

losing when
beginnings can end.

finding my
nothing in everything.

experiencing
reality,
for the very first time.

– *an introduction to oblivion*

what if
i've flown
so far
with
the wind,
i no longer
know
what it's like
to fly against it.

– *passive*

she
looked up
to the clouds
with half vigor
half sigh.
and decided
that day
she'd drink
from the sky.

– icarus

REBIRTH

he
was a
rainbow
who never met
a storm.

she
was a rose
who never grew
a thorn.

and together
they trekked
from the valleys
to the skies.
in search
of an elusive truth,
often veiled and disguised.

– rainflower

see her roots.

feel their foundation
and understand
you will never
uplift her.

deep down
somewhere between
your heart and soul
you will realize
you never wanted to,
anyway.

– *uplift*

i found
peace
in
chaos,
for
you
were
chaos.

– *chaotic peace*

i'd rather
be condemned
for loving too many
of the wrong things
than acclaimed
for hating
all the right.

– *love's damnation*

she
believed
in finding that
moment of eternity
that outlasts the past
endures the future
and reminds us
we are here
now

and that can never be taken away.

– eternal

as a poet

she
knew
not to cry.

for
her tears
bled to paper
memorialized
for all time.

and she
was so much more
than pain inked
across lines.

– *immortalized*

it
was
the moments
chained to reality

that maddened me the most.

– *poe's shackles*

she picked
daisies
from the sky
and placed them
back again at night.

for she knew
darkness
left alone
catches roots
and stakes a home.

– *beacon*

keep
dreaming
your dreams.
for it seems
that these dreams,
they bring
the most wondrous
of things.
things only redeemed
when dreamers
still dream.

– *forever dreams*

trust me
your love,
i'll give you
my heart.

in his
crimson blood,
he writes,
for she's art.

– muse

she transforms.

month to month
year to year
time immemorial.
red
white
green
yellow.
a cyclical dance.
always similar
but never the same.
how i wonder
is each new movement
growth from the previous?
or, as a phoenix,
rebirthed wholly anew?

– from the ashes

the audience –
silent.

her manager –
furious.

she –
didn't know what to feel.

should she have stayed on script?
remained quiet?
was she free,
or even more lost?

the lights began to dim.
curtains slowly closed.
she knew soon
she'd be yanked off stage.

the owner finally spoke –

"well...that's all folks."

a lone patron
stood and shouted –

"no, you misunderstood,
that's art she wrote."

– art cannot be silenced

she entered the train
pulled at her
fading flower dress
society insisted
was a biological
mismatch.

her eyes scanned
over each passenger
like a gazelle
before crossing
an open plain.

i wanted to say something –

you are loved.
you are strong.
you are worthy.

but when she
caught my eye,
it was her who silently
communicated to me –

you do
whatever enables you
to be the best
most true
version of you.

i wondered –

is this how
being naked felt
before the fall of man?

– eden

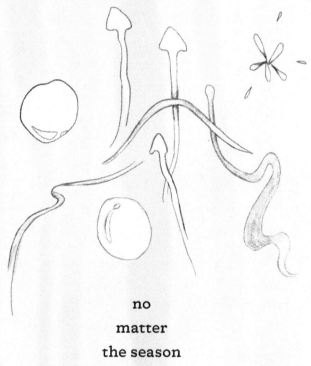

no
matter
the season
she'll rise
and
she'll shine.

– *effervescent*

whatever
you do
let
it
be
you.

– *you are your truth*